The Materialistic World

How to Escape Materialism, Theory of Materialism, Mindful Living, Living with True Happiness

Grace Scott

Copyright © 2014 by Grace Scott

All Rights Reserved

Disclaimer:

No part of this publication may be reproduced or transmitted in any form or by any means, or transmitted electronically without direct written permission in writing from the author.

While all attempts have been made to verify the information provided in this publication, neither the author nor the publisher assumes any responsibility for errors, omissions, or misuse of the subject matter contained in this eBook.

This eBook is for entertainment purposes only, and the views expressed are those of the author alone, and should not be taken as expert instruction. The reader is responsible for their own actions.

Adherence to applicable laws and regulations, including international, federal, state, and local governing professional licensing business practices, advertising, and all other aspects of doing business in the U.S.A, Canada or any other jurisdiction is the sole responsibility of the purchaser or reader.

Contents

Introduction

Chapter 1 - The Consequences of Materialism

Chapter 2 - How Much is Happiness?

Chapter 3 - Materialism and the Youth

Chapter 4 - The Remedy of Materialism

Chapter 5 - Non-Material Forms of Entertainment

Conclusion

Introduction

As the wheels of large corporations turn, everyday new and fancy products emerge into the market place creating a chasm of insatiable wants within every consumer. The desire to buy excessive items and to accumulate more tangible goods has been defined as materialism. The idea is neither new nor particular to the 21st century; rather, this malady has plagued individuals, societies and countries around the world. The desire to have, to possess, to own and to use has been seen in overwhelming proportions in the aristocracy around the world.

For the world as a whole, the distinction between intangible values like morality, honesty, justice and equality gradually became blurred. On the other hand, tangible objects like property, clothes, furnishings or vehicles had taken its place. Things which people could see represented wealth, affluence and status. Part of the reason for this shift in the value system was because material objects fascinated everyone. Be it the gleaming palaces of India, the gold thrones of Persia or the royal crown of Britain, extravagant objects became an emblem for everything that was good and desirable.

Another reason why materialism seeped into the minds was that the economic systems nudged people to be driven towards selfish motives. When self-interest became the rallying call, morality flew out the window. Cutthroat competition, an innate drive to excel and oppose others created distinctions between those who could succeed in this game and those who could not. Wealth is not intrinsically bad. But when people fail to distinguish between their wants and needs, excessive wealth becomes their own undoing.

Having possessions and owning private property provides a sense of security and insurance for most people and from this they also derive a sense of satisfaction and happiness. Happiness is generated directly from the preference satisfaction; if you can get instant gratification by purchasing something you desire for yourself or for someone else then there will be nothing which would make you happier.

Materialism is not merely a psychological condition; it is a state of mind and a state of one's lifestyle. For materialistic people pleasure is defined by sensory objects. i.e. those which could be touched, tasted, smelled, seen or heard. This is not to say that all materialistic individuals are devoid of feelings and emotions, it merely means that their epicurean desires drives them farther away from a universe which has highly sentimental and epistemic foundations.

To live a good life and to work hard are the principles couched even in the Protestant Ethic, but individuals are not aware of how to keep a balance in their wants and how to learn to deny themselves rather than plunging headlong into this hedonic abyss. When people become used to living in the moment and indulging their every desire, their wants keep on multiplying and they will transform themselves into a machine that either works for or swindles for the money required to fulfill those wants.

The constraint of money and resources is very real. Materialism numbs people to the harsher truths as they are socialized into thinking self-interest is the most important doctrine. Two major problems have ensued from such corrosive thinking; firstly, the desire for more money has led people to do illegal activities which bring the greatest income in the shortest time. Secondly, the fact that people have accumulated so many assets has created sharp social inequalities for those who still live under the poverty line.

It is odd to think that some people own so many unnecessary expensive items yet millions starve every day. This is only because materialism and self-interest have literally paralyzed their perception to value anything other than their wants. Charity or altruism will not fix these social quandaries because the individual mindset has to change.

Global poverty is not a single person's fault, but it is his or her responsibility because for every dollar you spend at one place, there are a million other places where it could have been spent. Materialism will not allow you to think beyond the box of your own self-love which is why people cannot learn to limit their desires.

When John Locke introduced the concept of private property, it was only to provide some sense of reward for hard labor. Hoarding relentlessly was considered unnatural in Locke's opinion. The rule of thumb was to take that which leaves enough for others. The idea was to make people considerate of the rights of every person in the society and not become land mongers.

Since the Industrial Revolution, developed countries have single-mindedly focused towards mass-production and sales. The psychological and human costs were not accounted for in this development race. Ideas like the American Dream had highly materialistic and avaricious roots which set a benchmark for people to aim towards, a standard which emphasized success and affluence. It was not surprising that materialism was synonymous with happiness and prosperity for the longest time.

But real prosperity came in terms of vast social divides and mindboggling statistics of inequality. The hunger to possess more things was basically the fuel for the capitalist machinery. Factories and corporations have made people believe that objects are the true representation for happiness. The mass media and large-scale advertisement, daily feed people images and ideas of things which they 'ought' to have but don't have at present.

However, thinking that the world is our birthright and its riches are up for grabs only instills a sense of plundering and looting until nothing except meaningless objects are exchanged and multiplied infinitely. A materialistic life is chaotic and restless because new desires and wants are created every second of the day and it isn't humanly possible or spiritually satisfying to hanker after our cravings.

As a result the noise of this continuous buying and selling has ratcheted up to a deafening cacophony where we are no longer attuned to appreciate or feel the finer things in life. According to the Journal of Consumer Research, materialism leads to social isolation and vice versa. This is true because people think that objects can be a suitable replacement for people. Such a form of self-absorption gradually became self-abnegation as people became victims of depression and loneliness.

This paralysis, where we want without thinking or knowing why, has decapitated all or perceptions of modesty and human dignity. Flowery displays of extravagance and smashing demonstrations of opulence have become commonplace. Luxurious mansions, several cars, glistening watches and jewels and numberless outfits make people feel that they are Croesus reincarnated.

An unhealthy reliance on wealth to create one's social stature makes people believe that they are nothing without their designer bags or shoes. According to a journal, Motivation and Emotion, "As people become more materialistic, their wellbeing (good relationships, autonomy, sense of purpose and the rest) diminishes. As they become less materialistic, it rises." In the present era, objects possess people rather than the reverse. People define themselves by how much they own and the sort of social circle they move in. Their life experiences, thoughts, reflections and lives are predetermined if they were born in a mansion or in a small shack. We live in an age where slavery has been redefined and the yoke is with our cars, gadgets, and shopping bags.

Materialism is simply a process that dehumanizes people and takes them on a journey of self-destruction where hedonism is more important than ethics. It is also socially repugnant because it divests people of their responsibilities and debars them from broadening their horizons to the intangible pleasures of life. Flaunting ones assets and getting appreciated for it, is not a plausible yardstick to judge a person with.

Humans are multidimensional, extremely capable creatures who contain the potential to move mountains, throwing away one's life and energies over things which won't last even a year seems unreasonable and irrational. In fact, those who pursue wealth and material possessions are the ones who end up feeling less satisfied and experience fewer positive emotions, because there will always be someone with something more and such a comparison will only instill an inferiority complex in people. Furthermore, anxiety and depression begins when there is a deep-seated, unconscious unhappiness. If people keep filling the void of their life with things it will always remain empty and meaningless.

There is a dire need to change the ideals and goals people have set for themselves as a society. This rat's race to collect as much as you can is asinine and time-consuming because people will spend most of their lives collecting things they will never use or need. Filling up shelves, garages, closets or cabinets is not the sole purpose of life. Notions of belonging to a family, having communal ties, being altruistic, reconnecting with nature brings people closer to the things that really matter in this short span of life. Objects would not build a personality or a character but self-esteem and diligence will shape your principles.

Chapter 1: The Consequences of Materialism

To stress on the idea that materialistic thinking is destructive, it is necessary to start this book with a thorough list of the consequences an individual will most likely face due to his or her materialistic behavior. This will help you, the reader, move on from a materialistic point of view to a more profound and non-materialistic appreciation of life. Before the cure for materialism can be discussed, its effects should be laid out:

Increased Debt Due to Heavy Borrowing

Many individuals are struggling to stay afloat now days because they are immersed in heavy debts. Debt is not accumulated automatically; people burden themselves with debts with their own will.

A lot of people are not in debt, yet they have everything they need. They are not necessarily considered wealthy, but they have a wise way of calculating what they need and what they want. They do not borrow money just to buy what they want or what they merely *think* they need.

In the same vein, if you are already struggling because many banks or loaning institutions are asking you to pay off your debts, it is time to take a different and better route.

Materialism will almost certainly pile up huge debts under your name. If the amount of cash flowing out of your pockets is greater than the amount of money flowing into your bank account, high debts are inevitable. If you do not have the means, it is best to avoid buying things that you do not need. You will give yourself a much-needed break from all the credit card bills if you stop buying things that will eventually just make your closet or home appear smaller.

The aforementioned can turn into a continuous cycle, and not everyone manages to get out of it, especially if they have never paused to reconsider their materialistic thinking. You must first accept that you need to stop concentrating on getting more material things, before you can determine the cure for your predicament. Only you can get yourself out of this pit.

Poor Self-Image

Obtaining expensive items may seem to be among the most effective instruments to boost one's confidence, but this is a deception of the mind. Unfortunately, materialistic thinking is greatly misguided and unfounded, despite how convincing it may feel. You can have the best-looking shoes in the room or the best home theater system in the neighborhood; however, these things won't help you develop genuine self-confidence, especially if you consider long-term self-esteem.

You will end up with a worsened self-image in the long run if you rely on material goods to prop up yourself, because you will be basing your greatness on things that can get worn out and are easily breakable. No matter how beautiful an object is, it will eventually get damaged and you might have to buy it again. If this particular object is not a necessity, you will also end up wasting money during this process. Many people try to use money to fill in a void in their identity, but this effort is inevitably in vain.

A time will come when your desire to have everything will significantly affect the way you carry yourself. You may not always have the financial capability to buy what you want, which will eventually give fuel to your frustrations. What if you do not have the newly-revealed clothing line of a world-renowned brand? What if you can't afford to buy brand new shoes to add to your large collection?

If you want to have a better and more beautiful self-image, do not build your confidence on material things. Instead, build your confidence on having a great character and healthy relationships. Also, you should foster confidence by developing yourself in ways that can positively contribute to the growth and happiness of others.

General Dissatisfaction

The term "new" can come to mind when one speaks of satisfaction. Yes, other concepts such as "efficient" and "durable" may also be considered, but many overestimate the satisfaction they receive from something brand new. People generally seek new things—new experiences and new relationships—and it is no secret that most would prefer to have a brand new mobile phone, car, and house rather than a used one.

Materialistic individuals are never satisfied, and this dissatisfaction can easily affect other areas of their lives. If you continue on the path of materialism, you won't find the satisfaction you are looking for. You will only have this constant desire to have what is new and better. A person may have just bought a smartphone a week ago, but if a new model has debuted since, he'll be subject to the strong urge to buy another one.

The same goes for people who follow the latest fashion trends. These individuals won't usually think twice about buying a shirt with a 4-digit price tag if it's the current trend. Satisfaction will certainly remain out of one's reach regardless, because materialism does not allow an individual to be satisfied. It just gives you a few drops of cold water as you traverse the hot desert. You simply won't ever have enough.

Hoarding

Many psychologists say that hoarding is a sign of an unhealthy viewpoint in life. Often, materialistic individuals are also hoarders, because they are not keen to let things go even if these can no longer be used. After all, according to hoarders, "more is better than less." In most cases, this principle is acceptable and practical. However, if you have a room full of clothes that you haven't worn for years, it's time to reconsider your principles.

When you hoard you also waste a great deal of money, which you should have used for other more important projects. Furthermore, you are wasting other precious resources. The air-conditioning or ventilation in your home will have to work extra hours because there are too many things absorbing the cold or warm air. Your utility bills will increase greatly, and once again, you will end up wasting money.

It doesn't matter how big your home is; hoarding has never been considered by most to be a healthy lifestyle. You have too many closets because you have too many clothes and shoes to keep track of. You may also have nearly every type of kitchen utensil—most of which you may have not used for quite some time. In this case, materialism is not just about one's wealth or financial capability—it's also about living in a practical manner. If you use only what you need, others will also have the chance to get what they need. You and your family are not the only people in the neighborhood and the world. Share resources with others and you will experience true satisfaction.

Compromised Aesthetics and Healthy Living Spaces

Some people think that a house's aesthetic appeal is not as important as having everything that you need. Quite the contrary; they are equally important. It's unwise to think that beauty must be sacrificed just to meet all your needs and wants. In the discussion of materialism, people are highly discouraged to continue buying or acquiring things that will just take more space in your home, consequently covering up every space. Your living space will become less appealing and, just as relevant, less healthy to live in.

This specific consequence of materialism will quickly impact nearly every aspect of your life. Many people say that "health is wealth," but what kind of health will you have if your home is only healthy for clutter and an abundance of possessions that you most likely do not need? If you think that by acquiring tangible goods you appear to be wealthy in the eyes of others, you are encouraged to think again.

You may have seen many home designs in various lifestyle magazines and noticed that a simple life is enough to have a beautiful home. You can still have everything you need, and some of the things you want, without negatively affecting the health of your family and the aesthetics of your home. Something that at first might seem to be a good indication of one's purchasing power and financial freedom can just as easily make an individual appear desperate and gravely disorganized.

Chapter 2: How much is Happiness?

To support the idea that materialism has more harmful effects than helpful and healthy ones, it's best to enumerate why it does not bring happiness. Happiness is one of the most essential requirements for any individual to live a fulfilling life. Everyone wants to be happy. This is one of the safest assumptions one can ever make. Some may claim to be masochistic, but their goal is to achieve happiness, even if their methods of attaining it are atypical. People look for ways to be happier, and many times they fail to find the right long-term sources of happiness. Materialism is not a viable genuine path to happiness and as you read on, you will discover why.

Someone Will Always Have More Than You

People who are materialistic are always looking for more and better items for themselves. Why? It's most likely because they have met someone who has a better phone, gadget, blouse, or TV than they do. Another probable reason is that the neighbor has more high-fashion clothing and more beautiful and more expensive furniture. The materialistic world is an ongoing war, one which won't end any time soon.

It's a fact of life that someone will always be better than you at something. It may be in the area of academics, corporate world performance, or the acquisition of what is "new" and "trending." If you constantly try to buy goods just to show that you are a better person than some of your "friends" and acquaintances, then you will just wind up frustrated. It's an unending war because it's a type of warfare where nobody wins. In the war of the materialists, no one can possibly win, because there is always something new to buy.

If you associate happiness with having the best and most lucrative goods, you will never be happy. If you somehow outdo a certain individual, someone else will come along and snatch the trophy away from you. Your triumph is short-lived, because you are not supposed to rely on just having material possessions to be happy. Genuine happiness comes from having the right relationships and being able to live life with passion and freedom. Do not be enslaved by materialism and money. Live your life without comparing yourself to others.

Material Things Get Worn out and are Breakable

You might possess a couple of brand new smartphones and might be very happy. You may even say that you are ecstatic because you have new "toys" to play with. However, what do you think you will happen a few months later? Do you think you will still have that excitement in your heart and sparkle in your eyes? You probably won't. Your brand new phones will no longer be new.

Material things do not last forever. They do not even last as long as you wish they would. The word "new" is accurately defined by using the word "old." If you base your happiness solely on an object, then your happiness will have an expiration date. It will neither last nor be helpful to your growth.

Maybe you are thinking, "but the guy at the shop said this phone is water-resistant and dust-resistant." Well, that may be true, but it can also get stolen. This is why people should never be reliant on objects as sources of happiness and satisfaction. If this is what you are going through, then your own happiness is at risk.

You will Just Wear out Yourself

It is very tiring to keep on buying things, especially if the frequency of purchases is constantly rising and the relevance of the products to your daily life is consistently dipping. At first, you may think it is fun to just buy things without any valid reason; however, you will gradually get tired because it all seems so pointless later on. You have nearly everything you could ever want, but you are not as happy as you thought you would be.

Materialism can never fill gaps in one's identity, which is why it can never be considered a good source of lasting happiness. People get tired and this exhaustion dries them up in every way possible. Remember that materialistic people aren't the only ones affected by their excessive spending and frequent shopping escapades. Their loved ones also suffer from their unhealthy inclinations. Basically, everyone gets tired, partly because there is too much stuff at home and cleaning becomes even more taxing.

Another reason why it's tiring to be materialistic is because you are urged to work harder just to fund your regular trips to malls and bazaars. You have to work overtime more often, because your current pay slip may not be enough to buy everything that you need. Do you think this is the lifestyle of a happy and satisfied individual? It's definitely not. Instead of spending your time with family and friends, you spend it at work. Your weekends are spent shopping, not bonding with loved ones. This cycle will wear you out faster than you think.

Your Character Will Be Compromised

People who possess the right character have a higher chance of becoming genuinely happy. It's because they have all the fundamental pillars that support a joyful existence. They see things in a sensible, practical, and positive manner, so they won't easily be beaten down if things do not turn out as they want. Materialistic individuals are far from being practical, sensible, and optimistic. Therefore, one can say that their character also needs to be developed.

Having the right attitude, which is produced by having a great character, is very important if you are after a lifetime of happiness. Your attitude determines how you deal with other people and how you react in various situations, whether they are good or bad. This means your relationships are also on the line as you try and sail the sea of materialism. Although the effects aren't as immediate as some may think, if you continue to focus on getting more and more each day, you will be considered a shallow individual.

Among the primary reasons why materialism should be ceased is its ability to adversely affect an individual from both the inside and outside. You will see cluttered and disorganized homes and offices, an obvious ill effect of materialism visible to any eye, but many lives are affected not because someone is spending too much time shopping, or has a cluttered space. It's simply because that person's changing into someone who's focused on getting things instead of establishing and taking care of his relationships and goals in life. If you have at least one reason to stop this materialistic journey, it's to preserve your character.

Chapter 3: Materialism and the Youth

It might be true that you are not a materialistic person at all, but it may be hard to say the same for your children, or the next generation. Many teens in the US have the financial capability, through their parents, to buy what they need and want. They also have a great deal of energy to shop. You could say that they are in a good shape and ideally positioned to spend money and be materialistic. While not all teenagers have sworn allegiance to materialism, many easily fall into the clutches of a materialistic viewpoint. If you want to know how teenagers are being affected by the strong wave of materialism, this will prove to be the most influential chapter.

Low Probability of Working Hard

When adolescents become extremely materialistic, they tend to lose zealousness and passion for many other things. It's not that they suddenly lose the skills to accomplish the tasks assigned to them, or that they do not like what they are doing. Rather the problem is that, since they are solely focused on getting things, they will only pay attention to issues that can help them get what they want. It could be a new smartphone, laptop, tablet, shoes, shirt, or any other material thing which they consider to be precious.

In general, teens have become lazy, because if they are not rewarded with a brand new "toy" or the latest clothing line, they won't do what they are told. They become overgrown children and they won't be driven enough to accomplish great feats. Even though they are just teenagers, they can contribute positively and significantly to the world, or at least, to their own community.

Once they have acquired what they have been "dreaming" of, they will stop working as hard as they once did. They stick to short-term goals because these are relatively easy to achieve. Since they are behaving in such a way during adolescence, it's likely they will behave in the same way once they are older. They will only exert more effort at the office because they are saving up for that brand new phone or a more advanced laptop or game console. Their finish lines are too close to the starting line, preventing them from becoming fighters, and rendering them mere 50-meter dash racers who cease to train once they get their trophy in hand.

Low Self-Esteem as the Root and the Fruit

A 2006 study conducted by marketing professors at the University of Illinois showed that children with low self-esteem have a higher chance of becoming materialistic. The kids with low self-esteem use material items to produce happiness, but children with high self-esteem gained happiness through friendships, playing, being great at sports, and by helping others.

Parents can't blame materialism on the advertisers or on the media alone. As parents or guardians, they are responsible for their own children's character-development.

Low self-esteem can also be the fruit of materialism. Even if a teenager was once confident, if he eventually associates his importance or greatness as an individual with the things he possesses, it will be a pretty quick trip to having an inferiority complex. He won't always have the latest or the best, and once he realizes this, he will be depressed and have low self-esteem. Materialism is an evil gardener. It plants a weed that may look like a harmless plant, but this plant will just waste the nutrients in the soil and choke the other plants around it. Materialism will destroy a person's life, and it can ruin a teen's life, even faster as compared to an adult's, as teens are so much more impressionable and sensitive to the opinions of their peers.

Misdirected and Meaningless Goals

Teenagers are primarily focused on fitting in, and not planning on having a great future. They do not focus on performing well in school and in other community programs because they are not going to get that new phone they have wanted. They are concerned about their image and they will do just about anything to preserve and improve that good image. Even at such a young age, these individuals have firmly established the desire for material goods, which is quite troubling.

It's not that most teenagers do not have goals, but the goals they will share with others do not often appear to be aims that will have a long-term positive effect on their lives and on the people around them. Adolescents need all the guidance and help they can get. Unfortunately, they won't admit that they need assistance, particularly when they are too busy thinking of what to buy next and how they can buy them.

It's the parent's responsibility to make sure that their children's fundamental viewpoints in life are built on a good and sensible foundation. It's not going to be an easy battle to win against materialism. With guidance and awareness, these materialistic young individuals can still be reformed. It takes time and effort, but it's not an impossible task.

Unethical Behavior

The November 2011 edition of the *Scientific World Journal* contained a research paper which found a third of materialistic teens in Hong Kong would actually consider engaging in unethical activities just to get money to buy what they want. Such unethical behavior included being a companion for money. Surprisingly, 34 percent of the survey respondents said they would seriously consider that option. Out of the 34 percent of teens who were already engaging in "compensated dating," nearly 17 percent got into a sexual relationship.

Being materialistic is already considered unethical by the general population, because as we already know that money and material possessions can't give us sustainable happiness. Of course, more unethical behavior will stem from materialistic inclinations and compulsions. This goes for each and every one of us, not only teenagers. In time, the desperation or intense desire to get new things will lead a person to do what he thought he could never do. Ethics and character are thrown out of the window because materialism has entered the house.

Chapter 4: The Remedy of Materialism

Although prevention is better than cure, the remedy for materialism should still be known. Now that you are more familiar with the consequences of materialism and how it impacts the lives of each and every person no matter what age group they are in, you are ready to be receptive to the cure. Indeed, you may have finally begun considering some form of solution to address the problem of materialism. Fortunately, there's more than one way to get away from materialism. The strategies provided below are not only effective, but also simple and easy to do. You will understand the different types of exits you can take as you read along.

Become Environmentally Conscious

The environment has the ability to naturally heal itself. What it can't do, however, is outpace the harmful and selfish activities of men and women. The fast-paced and highly materialistic lifestyle of the world is seriously adversely affecting the planet. You may think this is just another reminder to go green, but the issue of environmental preservation and the elimination of materialistic behavior are closely related. This is why carbon footprints are measured.

If a person is materialistic, his carbon footprint is most likely larger than that of another individual who's not. Your contribution to the planet's deterioration is closely linked to your consumption. The more you purchase, consume, and utilize, the more industries or companies have to produce. Since demand is so high, the production must keep up. This essentially means that the more materialistic people become, the faster the destruction of the environment will be.

Make an effort to recycle or reuse things even if you think that buying a few new things won't make much of a difference. Every small act counts and helps. By having your broken toaster repaired instead of getting a new one, you save money and time. You do not have to go on a trip to the mall just to get a new one, and while there, be tempted to buy several other things which you may not need. You also help to save the environment by not having so much stuff to throw away. Since your home won't be filled with so many things, you will also avoid throwing a lot of things away in the future, in your attempts to de-clutter. It is certainly a win-win situation; both you and the environment win.

Avoid Watching Too Much Television

When you watch television, you are inevitably exposed to numerous advertisements. Those dreaded home shopping networks really know how to make something look very appealing. Many take the bait and are eventually face to face with a bunch of things they do not really need. Yes, salespeople have one job: to sell a product. There are many people who are quite good at selling things. At times, even if an average guy is hesitant to buy a bottle of shampoo, a seasoned salesperson can effortlessly change his mind.

This does not have to be the case for you, though. You can avoid getting into such situations if you choose to not be exposed to them. Although there are door-to-door salespeople, who are also good at selling various products, you can considerably decrease your chances of making unnecessary purchases if you turn the television off and find other ways to be entertained. Once again, effort is needed in doing this and changing your lifestyle to a less materialistic one, but you will find it is well worth it.

Even if you are not watching many commercials or product presentations, you are still vulnerable to the influence of the media. Businesses will use each and every opportunity to sell their products to you because that's the only way their income can increase. It's natural for them to do their best to make every product as enticing as possible. However, it shouldn't be natural for buyers to immediately respond to every ad with a troubling level of excitement, eager for another purchase. It may be the job of advertisers to promote their products, but it's the responsibility of consumers to be wise, careful, and collected when considering buying a product.

Avoid Excessive Web-Surfing

In essentially the same way as outlined in the prior section, consumers are encouraged to avoid surfing the web too often. The World Wide Web has increasingly become the top advertising instrument for most businesses across the globe. You will deal with a surplus of pop-up ads, site banners, and online product offers that can easily render the average person's strong will useless. If you are materialistic, internet-surfing will definitely be one of your greater Achilles' heels.

Since globalization is now an apparent reality, even the dissemination of information regarding certain products and the shipping or delivery of said objects has become easier. Unfortunately, this also means that the process of becoming materialistic, or being even more consumed by materialism, is growing ever simpler. The internet is a helpful source of information, but it can also be an ally of materialism. You should not let yourself be exposed to many online ads. Materialism can be cured, and staying away from the internet for a while will help you to do so.

Consider Buying Used Appliances

Garage sales are ideal sources of much-needed furniture, fixtures, clothing, and other things. You do not always have to buy new things, but this doesn't mean you should buy just anything. You will surely need to buy brand new clothes every now and then, for example. Fortunately, you can often find several used (but beautiful and very wearable) outfits at various bazaars and garage sales, lessening the amount of times you have to buy new clothes. Ideally, you won't just be doing this because they are cheaper, but because you are also helping other people out in so many ways.

For instance, the family that's selling their sofa may really need the money to help pay some of their bills. The sofa still looks great, and it's also a good bargain. Materialistic individuals are generally drawn towards new and pricey things, but wise and controlled shoppers buy what they can use without thinking about how much they can brag about its price tag or where they bought it to others. Prioritize function, and then proceed to aesthetics.

Stop Considering Shopping as a Recreational Activity

Shopping is not a sport. You can never put "frequent and fast shopper" on your résumé, because it is not a skill! It's only an occasional activity. You may shop with your friends and relatives. But still, if you shop too often, it's a sign of being materialistic. You need to stop considering shopping as a recreational activity.

If you want to cure your materialism, stay out of the mall for a long time and look for other ways to "entertain" yourself. You can opt to do this on your own—soul-searching or a one-person road trip—or with your loved ones. You can have fun, learn new skills, and even meet new people. When you shift your focus from shopping every week, you will start experiencing real joy, which it's something money can't buy.

Declutter

Another important cure that you may require or find useful is decluttering. Decluttering is one of the most liberating things you can do for yourself. It may seem intimidating at first, but it will become easier once you get started and the more often you do it.

Your home or living space directly affects the way you get in or out of a materialistic point of view. A clean home is a clear sign of a healthy family. It's also an indication that you are very serious about not letting your material possessions consumes you and your family. This is a crucial step, particularly when your home has become one big stock room. Your clothes are filling each drawer, your tools are placed in various odd places, and your furniture can't even be seen under the piles of things you have bought. It's time to clean things up and throw away stuff you do not need.

Remember, the more you consume, the more you become enslaved by your belongings. This is also why we should always reconsider when we are purchasing something that is not a "need".

Chapter 5: Non-Material Forms of Entertainment

This chapter aims to elaborate on the best strategy you can use to get started taking part in non-material forms of entertainment. The things enumerated here may not be considered a complete list of things you can do to entertain yourself in a non-material fashion. These are the top ways in which many people have proven to be effective and quite easy to put in action. You can start doing many of these activities right now.

Nature and Meditation

Nature has a way of transforming an individual, and it's among the most reliable sources of peace and happiness. As you wait for the sun to set, you get this wonderful feeling of accomplishment knowing that another day has passed by and you spent it reveling in life and the blessings you have received. These are not necessarily material blessings, but may instead be the gift of time, energy, good health, and great relationships.

Many people meditate regularly, not merely because they are big fans of Kung Fu movies, but because they are after a greater awareness of what's actually important. Nature can help you see that many things you are after in this life may not be helpful to your long-term growth and improvement as an individual and as a member of the society. Very few realize the truth that material things take much more than what they give. You may have a lot of material possessions, but what about the other aspects of your life?

What about your performance as an employee, business owner, student, parent, and friend? Life isn't just about amassing what you think you need to be happy or about getting what you really want. It's about discovering the frailty of the material and the beauty of the abstract. Simply put, do not focus too much on getting the latest gadget or having a well-stocked and up-to-date wardrobe. Take a look at nature. It's so simple, yet it can easily take one's breath away. The best things in life do not come from the mall or from the delivery guy—they come from what naturally surrounds you.

Spend time with Your Family and Friends

Spending time with your family will help fill the gaps in your soul, gaps which you once tried to fill through excessive shopping or a troubling degree of materialism. Your family is, and should be, the primary source of your happiness, because that's what they are there for. The time you spend with your loved ones will surely bring about lasting joy, and later on in your life, you won't regret a single minute or second that you spent with your parents, children, and other relatives.

It's likely that no one has ever said on their deathbed that they should have shopped more and gained more riches. When you spend time with your family, it's like you are giving them a well-wrapped gift, which they can never get from anyone else. This present is so unique because it is your time. No one can turn back time; and if you have read Mitch Albom's *The Time Keeper*, you will see that the best moments in life are the ones spent with those you love, not in any bazaar or mall.

Have a serious or fun conversation with your parents, ask your kid what he's been up to lately, or play a board game with other relatives. It's these moments in life that can never be bought by money. These times are priceless and precious. Unfortunately, they do not come as often nowadays because of the fast-paced and materialistic lifestyle many people have adopted. You can change your ways, and can certainly be a better member of your family. You can still buy things in moderation, but make sure that the time you are spending with your family is not compromised.

Read a Book

Reading a book is also a good way to entertain yourself. Many people fail to see the limitless creative and interesting ideas books bring to their readers. Readers become equipped with the necessary knowledge, insight, and versatility to go on with each day and be happy no matter what they have in their hands. Do not belittle the power of reading; most of the greatest minds in recent centuries, and even in this generation, got to where they are through a book.

Books may be material possessions—unless you just borrowed them—but the point here is that they can be used to keep your mind occupied and to keep the creative juices in your head flowing. You will have so much fun flipping through the pages of a good paperback if you just allow yourself to get into the experience. You do not have to spend money on a ton of things just to remain mentally active. If you want mental exercise, and a very fun way to spend a couple of hours each day, grab a good book and read.

Explore Other New Places

The world is one big hodge-podge of different places, cultures, and people. Instead of filling your house, hands, and wardrobe with things that you will eventually give or throw away, just spend your hard-earned money to learn more about the world you are in. Many things can surprise you and you will certainly think that you have spent your money well. Learning about different regions and meeting new friends in your journey will greatly increase the uniqueness of your identity.

You will become more confident as you try and learn how to adjust in different countries or states. You won't need a new high-fashion purse, clothing, or any other material things just to show others that you are great. Your perspective of the world changes and grows. Do not hesitate to explore what's beyond your own back- or front-yard. The world is for you to see because it is your home. Get to know it more and you will definitely be far from becoming materialistic.

Get to Know Your Neighbors

It's somehow silly to think that some individuals do not know many people in their own neighborhood. They have been too busy buying things and strolling around shopping centers or bazaars that they are unable to meet potential friends. As many would say, "No man is an island." Even if you have every single material object you have ever wanted, if you do not have any friends to share them with, life would be quite empty.

Every single day is an opportunity to meet new friends and be more connected in the community you are in. There will be a time when you will need the aid or support of your neighbors, so try spending some time to get to know them and have some engaging conversations. Do not let them think that you are simply not sociable or friendly. They may think you are just too concerned about getting more things into your home, but you have the chance to show them that you care about them as well.

The more friends you have, the more you will be spending time with them. This means you will have less time running around in the mall every week or every day just to get the latest clothing, appliances, and many other "things". Since you have more people in your life who can help you see life in a better light, you won't think too much about getting that new cellphone or that new jeans you saw the other day. Once you are connected to people, you will consequently be disconnected with materialistic things.

Conclusion

The ceaseless accumulation of objects is neither economically nor socially viable because most of the items purchased are never used. Hoarding in such a manner costs a lot as people are determined to buy things which are in fashion so newer and newer models keep emerging to entrap people in this vicious cycle of impulse buying. Advertising makes individuals believe that possessing objects is a symbol of status and if they do not have the latest model of a cell phone, a car or some other gadget they will probably fall down the social ladder. Accumulation of items is then equated to one's position in the society. Not surprisingly, objects are used to inspire awe in others and to further one's way into different elitist social circles.

These items also become a tool for entry into exclusive cliques as the only way people will allow someone to enter is if they possess all the expensive paraphernalia. Exclusivity and the need to maintain a distinction is perhaps the greatest motivation for materialists. Their clothes and belongings give them a distinctive air of grandeur; it makes them feel better about their self-image since these items represent their power and status.

As a result, a materialist can easily gain access into an elite group and interact with others who have similar interests. Materialists would rarely stoop below their illusionary stature to interact with those who do not share similar interests. Therefore, interaction happens with those who possess similar assets, for example people living in a certain highbrow, expensive residential area might only interact amongst each other. Such materialistic individuals interact with those who are 'lower' than their social status in order to extract patronage and appreciation. Praise is almost fundamental in perpetuating materialism since it provides a legitimacy to people's actions and they end up thinking excessive buying and amassing of things is the right approach to build up one's social standing.

Socially materialism is a malady for it is the reason behind such severe boundaries of class and status. It effectively puts people into these compartments of poverty and wealth and society judges their character and worth through the things they own. As a result the people who are at the bottom of the social ladder are consistently oppressed and trapped into this net of poverty because wealth is solidified at the top tiers and it never trickles down to benefit anyone else in the society. Social responsibility and morality are completed undermined by such a behavior. As impulse buying becomes an addiction, people develop a sense of indifference towards the suffering of others. Such heightened social aloofness results in crime and dissatisfaction at every level of the society.

The harsh reality is that wealth is being created only through oppression and exploitation of weaker groups in the society. Low wages, unsafe working conditions and long working days lead to the creation of wealth for the upper classes. Socially responsible individuals would realize how capitalists exploit the poor to benefit the rich, but materialists are so engrossed in their own world of bags and clothes that they cannot comprehend the millions of lives put at risk.

Materialism allows capitalism to pervade every strata of the society. The creation of wealth is unfair because it pitches the 99% against the 1% who own enormous amounts of assets around the world.

Such an arrangement is neither ethically nor democratically fair because the 1% of the globe is effectively usurping the rights of the 99%. It is true that today we have more assets and we consume more than we did 50 years ago, but it is also true that crime, disease, depression, hunger and poverty has increased exponentially. Materialism is economically inefficient because the scarce resources of this world are being used to create things which people do not even use. For running of large industries every day we are using up our natural resources and depleting them only to feed the never ending gluttony of the hedonists.

The global reserves of fossil fuels, clean water and even clean air are being rapidly consumed to feed industrial giants. This makes one wonder if everyone learns to control their wants and to desire what they need then most of the global problems would not have existed. Even politically groups contend to possess more resources and wars are waged for precisely continuing the production process in developed economies.

In consequence it is not surprising why people are still not happy and content perhaps this is because real contentment cannot be derived through objects.

As mentioned earlier one of the most alarming result of materialism is the widespread dissatisfaction it generates.

Materialism closely mimics the trends and fads currently propagated by mass media, therefore, in reality there is no limit to what people can buy and possess during their lifetime but they are constrained by their budget, physical abilities, age or even regional location and this creates an inherent sense of frustration and discontentment. The problem persists because the starting point of an overly great reliance on objects was flawed.

Materialistic people fail to realize that things are merely transient and transitory and that they will not last forever. Therefore, basing one's life, energies and aspirations on such a shaky foundation seems asinine. Such people also find it exceedingly hard to deal with the loss of their belongings, for instance, during a natural calamity or economic downturn. People cannot handle issues like bankruptcy, political downfalls or any other loss in their social stature and more often than not they end up mentally ill.

Materialism actually incapacitates people and makes them weaker because they rely on their assets to act as a bulwark against everything. They are not mentally or physically equipped to deal with anything other than luxury. People who build up their self-image on the foundation of objects are committing a grave mistake.

Another interesting aspect of materialism is its synonymy with happiness which is an extremely flawed perception. It is true that the fulfillment of desires makes people happy but this happiness is short lived because the completion of one desire means the creation of another. Such a system traps people into this cycle where they expend their energies in acquiring more things every day. These individuals can never be happy with their present state because there is always some new object in the market which they don't have.

This is physically and mentally tiring for them because they search for the elusive happiness in items which will get worn off or broken with the passage of time. Happiness remains unattainable because no one actually pauses to reflect on what they have and there is no gratitude for all the blessings of wealth and health they possess. Instead these blessings are considered to be their legal right and they can never appreciate the importance of what they have. Similarly looking at others who have more than them also decreases their happiness because they feel a sense of material deprivation.

Materialism is a race in which no one will ever win. The richest person of the world may have nothing more to his or her credit than the amount of money they possess. The scale through which people assess each other is derogatory because it downplays the importance of human character. The goodness of one's self is not important compared to hundreds of items lying in a closet. Ideas like social justice, equality and empathy dwindle in the face of the love for material objects.

Undoubtedly, a society is not held by the amount of cars and cellphones its individuals possess but by the strength and substance of its norms and value. Materialism is therefore, creating a generation of highly indifferent, self-interested and immoral individuals who will be ready to do anything for wealth.

Youngsters are afflicted by this phenomenon where gathering objects is more important than improving one's life and reflecting on the world.

It is extremely saddening that today's generation is devoid of experiencing finer emotions of connecting with the universe, nature and humanity as a whole. Even if they do something good they continuously feel the need to garner praise for it and to preserve it in form of photographs. Materializing everything is their primary aim in life and experiencing sentiments and appreciating the vagaries of this universe is inconsequential. For them life would not hold any meaning as they are searching for it in the wrong place. Most individuals of today's young generation are sadly bereft of the capacity of self-awareness and self-actualization.

In essence materialism is a social, economic and psychological problem which is destroying our reality and rotting our morality. The race to acquire more items must stop because it is a never ending, exhaustive process which will sap us of all higher sentiments. The solution would be to concentrate on things other than objects and to explore different avenues of life like reading, spending time in nature, doing selfless act and so on.

Empathy for others will also help in making people realize that so many objects are not essential to lead a happy life because there are millions of people around the world living with much less. Meditation and reconnection with our spiritual needs will also help bridge this gap of satisfaction.

In conclusion, in order to rid our society of materialism, there is a need for positive role models and a complete paradigm shift. Understanding the problem of materialism and being aware of its serious psychological and social repercussions will make people more responsible in their decision-making. Our choices as individuals or groups should be motivated by ethical and moral rules rather than an impulsive desire to multiply our wealth. The purpose of this book was to demonstrate the negative ramifications of engaging in the self-centered pursuit of materialism, which can ultimately numb one's senses towards ideas like empathy and altruism. It successfully proves that materialism is not sustainable as a lifestyle because we are social beings who are driven by motives that might go against our personal desire for material assets.

The cornerstone of judicious and prudent living is to focus on the immaterial and realize the deeper nuances of the choices we make and their consequences on our lives and lives of those around us. Every time you are driven to possess something, pause and reflect on the number of beneficiaries of that decision, think about the alternative uses of your money and carefully consider the consequences of your decision; taking a comprehensive approach for reassessing your wants and needs will steer you towards healthy living.

Thank you for reading "The Materialistic World".

I sincerely hope that you received value from this and gain a better understanding of the consequence of materialism, its effects, and remedies.

If you enjoyed this book, please take a moment to share your thoughts and leave a review on Amazon, even if it's only a few lines; it would make all the difference and would be very much appreciated!

Thank you and good luck!

Grace Scott

Lightning Source UK Ltd.
Milton Keynes UK
UKHW02f1912240918
329454UK00027B/1523/P